THE
FORGOTTEN SHIPWRECK

'Lost with all hands'

The tragic loss of the Greek ship 'Flag Theofano'
and her 19 crew in Solent waters

Front cover photos: *Flag Theofano* after conversion in 1989
Photo: Unknown source

Life ring photos: Author

Sonar image of the wreck on the seabed…Author

Copyright: Martin Woodward 2022

ISBN: 978-0-9552916-3-0

Published by Coco Design Co Publishing
4 Bucks Cottages, Kingston Road,
Shorwell, Isle of Wight. PO30 3LP

E-mail: simone.dickens@gmail.com

Printed by Book Printing UK, Remus House,
Coltsfoot Drive, Woodston, Peterborough, PE2 9BF

'In memory of the crew of Flag Theofano'

CONTENTS

FOREWORD

Pondering Flag Theofano

The waters of Wight and Solent conceal a graveyard of foundered and forgotten craft. A popular map of Wight shipwrecks, by '*Planaship*', identifies some 300, and these are only the ones that have been named and noted in records of the past few centuries.

Marine salvage claims an early history in the dark Guinness-coloured waters of the Solent. It is here that 'Jacob the Diver' (1627) and brothers John and Charles Deane (1829-1840) made pioneer descents to the seabed while pitching their trust in rudimentary and home invented diving apparatus. Whatever they saw from the brass helmet or the diving bell, might only be conveyed with a brush, a pen and some help from the engraver's imagination. For pioneers such as these, it seems that the event of ship-loss had inevitably stirred that latent human desire to seize some modicum of consolation from a seafarer's tragedy and failure.

In many respects, our maritime history presents a perceptible progression in which the power of the sea has been first attributed to fearsome gods, and then to a natural and turbulent force that should ever demand the greatest respect. Since our marine engineering and satellite technologies have advanced, the sea has now become an exploitable resource that we seek to manage within varying levels of international discord. The sewage and plastic dross, shifting on our shoreline, bears testimony to our failure.

During the past fifty years, human activity on the seabed has advanced from salvage to science, sport and recreation, while the event of a ship-loss still holds its timeless and uncompromising threat. Produced in the 1990s, an overview by the Royal Commission on Historical Monuments has charted a remarkable galaxy of historic shipwrecks surrounding Britain's coast. A closer view reveals specific concentrations in the waters of the Thames, Solent and the Bristol Channel. Like a fly in amber, here is transfixed physical evidence of past lives and events; a record that is still accruing.

When do these lost craft graduate from an actuary's assessment of a lost investment, to an historic entity that begs its own particular regard? When we turn to the tragedy of the *Flag Theofano,* we realise that the night of January 29th, 1990 was the very moment when a new and permanent entry was made in the seabed's hidden archive of maritime and social history.

When Pliny the Younger wrote of the eruption of Vesuvius in AD 79, he brought vital testimony to a unique and catastrophic event in which two great cities and their populations were disastrously encapsulated in a single rapid event. Today, it is Pliny's words and a sunken discovery that has brought a long-forgotten world back to life. When Martin Woodward leads us through the events surrounding *Flag Theofano's* night-time tragedy, we very soon realise how a disastrous event in the lives of crew and families may slip into undeserved oblivion.

Fortunately, in this account of a virtually forgotten ship, we are guided by one of the foremost investigators of both modern and historic wrecks. The Woodward archive and a lifetime's assembly of artefacts, endows us with the unique privilege of pondering the magnitude of the Solent's seabed legacy. While random trophy-hunting, auctioning and dispersal has plagued so many of Britain's nearshore wrecks, here we meet with sustained determination to curate and display all, in the Isle of Wight Shipwreck Centre and Maritime Museum.

In this investigation of the *Flag Theofano* we meet with many of the vicissitudes that ever shadow a crew at sea. Here is no place for a reader's schadenfreude, for our guide surely empathises with this event in a manner that gently reminds us that every lost ship carries its own unique story as it passes into the underwater archive of the seabed. Here we gain a rare privilege of learning of the final resting place of this ship as seen, directly, through the author's diving mask and viewfinder. Now that the recent loss and wreck of *Flag Theofano* has been examined in such remarkable detail, we can only eagerly await more of Martin Woodward's investigations on the floor of Sea Area Wight.

Dr David Tomalin, FSA.

(Visiting Professor, University of Southampton, Centre for Maritime Archaeology)

PREFACE

Very few people are aware of the sad story of the *Flag Theofano* and the loss of all 19 of her crew on 29th January 1990. This tragedy took place within Solent waters just over three miles off Bembridge and four miles off Hayling Island.

The story quickly disappeared into the mists of time and has been virtually forgotten, even though the wreck marker buoys are visible from both sides of the Solent. Hopefully, this small publication will help in paying tribute to the lost crew, 14 of who are still entombed inside the wreck. Four of the five bodies that were washed ashore were repatriated to their home countries for burial, but a young Maldivian seaman named Ibrahim Hussain remained in the UK and was buried in an unmarked grave in Portsmouth. Thankfully in 2022, this was remedied with the installation of an engraved headstone, along with an appropriate commemoration service. Southampton Shipowners Association have also kindly sponsored a memorial plaque to be placed at Holyrood Church, Southampton, which was built in 1320 and in 1957 dedicated as a memorial to the sailors of the Merchant Navy. There will also hopefully be a *Flag Theofano* memorial plaque installed in the new Eastney sea defences in 2023/24, forming part of the latest Southsea Coastal Scheme. Portsmouth City Council are kindly looking into the possibility of achieving that. Additionally, I have created a small memorial and engraved plaque at the bottom of my garden adjacent to the sea wall overlooking the *Flag Theofano's* final resting place off

Bembridge. Hopefully, these memorials will keep the story of the tragedy alive, and I will mention all those involved in these kind acts in the Acknowledgements section at the end of this book. It is heart-warming to see the recent renewed interest in the *Flag Theofano* tragedy some 32 years after she was lost.

Headstone for Ibrahim Hussain Photo: Steve Hunt

Memorial in author's garden at the sea wall overlooking the site of the wreck Photo: Author

Please note that the conclusions and assumptions in this account of the sinking are based on all the evidence I gathered whilst I was carrying out diving and sonar surveys for the MAIB (Marine Accident Investigation Branch) and *Flag Theofano's* owners and insurers immediately after the sinking on 29th January 1990. I acquired all the evidence detailed below between February and May 1990, and this was all submitted in written reports at the time. Additionally, I carried out further sonar imaging and diving in 2022 to confirm the position of various pieces of outlying wreckage from the ship. These other items of wreckage included the after goalpost masts that had impacted the seabed and broken off while the ship was dragging almost upside down and semi-buoyant to its final sinking position. Although previously visible on my 1990 sonar images, these additional pieces of outlying wreckage were again re-confirmed by more recent sonar technology.

I emphasise again that the conclusions below are my own opinions based on the logical sequence of events surrounding the tragic sinking of the *Flag Theofano.* Any criticisms, conflicting views, or new evidence would be welcomed and, if appropriate, corrected in future reprints of this book.

All photographic sources are credited where known, but any unknown sources will be corrected and credited if informed before any future reprints. I apologise for my amateurish sketches and artworks of the timeline and other evidence, but it seemed the easiest way to explain the sequence of events.

Martin Woodward MBE

Bembridge, Isle of Wight

May 2022

Flag Theofano after 1989 conversion. (Photo source unknown)

FLAG THEOFANO

'The Forgotten Shipwreck'

Vessel details:

Builder: Martin Jansen GmbH & Co. KG Schiffsw. U. Masch…Leer. Yard No. 94 in 1970. Germany

Length Overall: 99 metres, beam 14.1 metres

Gross Tonnage: 2812 tons : Deadweight 4470 tons

Machinery: 2 Oil engines geared to screw shaft driving single fixed pitch propellor.

Total Power: Mcr 2, 648kW (3600hp)- Service speed 14 knots

Prime Mover Detail: Design: MWM, Engine Builder: Motoren Werke Mannheim AG (MWM), West Germany- 2x TBRHS345SU 4 Stroke, Single Acting, Inline, (Vertical- 6 cal 360 x 450, Mcr: 1324 kW -1800hp at 500 rpm)

Aux Generators: 3x160kW 380V 50Hz a/c, 2x 40kW 380V 50Hz a/c

Fuel Bunkers Capacity: 452 tonnes

Vessel Call sign: SYGJ

Vessel History:

1970: Launched 10/01/70 ID 7010107 'Boston Express' Owners: P/R Boston Express, Port Kiel

1970: Name change to 'Ino'

1971: Name change to 'Ino A'

1974: Name change to 'Rabat' Change of owners to Sea Malta Co Ltd. Port: Valletta, Malta

1980: Name change to 'Victoria' Change of owners to Cilicia Sg Co.SA: Port: GRC Piraeus

1989: Name change to 'Flag Theofano' Change of Owners to Seawave Cia Naviera SA: Piraeus

1989: Sold to Golden Union Shipping Co. May 1989: Conversion to bulk cement carrier

1989: End of July, completion of refit and the ship sailed from Piraeus Dockyard

1989: August. First trip to Southampton with bulk cement cargo.

1990: January 29th: Capsized after cargo shift on 21st voyage to Southampton. Crew of 19 all lost. 11 Greek, 7 Maldivian, 1 Egyptian

Flag Theofano as 'Victoria' 1980-1989

The Crew:

Captain/Master: Pittas, Ioannis, Age 44. Greece (Body found 30/01/90)

Chief Officer: Papastamatiou, Isidoros, Age 37. Greece

2nd Officer: Skaltsaris, Hariton, Age 28. Greece (Body found 30/01/90)

Radio Officer: Frangos, Nikolaos, Age 36. Greece (Body found 16/02/90)

Chief Engineer: Marinakis, Georgios, Age 31. Greece

3rd Engineer: Mpiskas, Agelos, Age 50. Greece

3rd Engineer: Hagias, Ioannis, Age 43. Greece

Electrician: Petsas, Apostolos, Age 46. Greece

Bosun: Gatanas, Pantelis, Age 34. Greece (Body found 14/02/90)

Apr/Engineer: Skiathitis, Leonidas, Age 23. Greece

Cook: Pappazis, Georgios, Age 40. Greece

Oiler: Said, Badr, Age 40. Egypt

A.B: Ali-Ibrahim, Waheed, Age 38. Maldives

A.B: Mohamed, Naeem, Age 33. Maldives

A.B: Hussain, Ibrahim, Age 19. Maldives (Body found 19/02/90)

Deck Boy: Didi, Ali, Age 19. Maldives

Oiler: Ibrahim, Adam, Age 25. Maldives

Asst. Steward: Abdulah, Niyam, Age 21. Maldives

Asst. Cook: Rasheed, Mohamed, Age 18. Maldives

Flag Theofano after 1989 conversion. Source unknown

THE STORY

One of the worst local shipping disasters of recent times occurred on 29th January 1990 when the 2812 ton Greek cargo ship *Flag Theofano* capsized and sank only 3.5 miles off Bembridge, Isle of Wight, during the night. It was her 21st trip to Southampton's Western Docks, Berth 108. All 19 crew sadly perished that night.

The seas were still very heavy from the severe storm 4 days previously, with ongoing Force 8-9 SSW winds and a significant swell running through the English Channel. The *Flag Theofano* was on a voyage from Le Havre to Southampton with a cargo of 3920 tons of bulk cement, and on approaching the Nab Tower at 1730hrs had called Southampton VTS and given her ETA at the Nab Tower as 1945 hrs, requesting a pilot to enter port. She reported again when passing the Nab Tower at 1923 hrs after achieving an average speed of 10.5 knots since leaving Le Havre. Due to appalling weather conditions causing docking delays, she was instructed to anchor in the shelter of St Helens Roads until a pilot was available to safely board the vessel and proceed into Southampton. That was the last communication received from the vessel, despite later calls from the pilot station and Niton Radio during the night.

It was not until a ship's lifeboat with the *Flag Theofano's* name on was found washed ashore at the east end of Hayling Island next morning that the alarm was raised. Two bodies were also found washed ashore close by at West Wittering and the rescue services rapidly swung into action. The pilot launch, with a

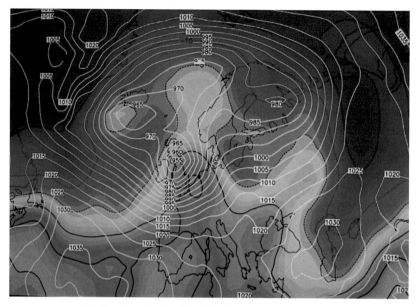

Weather chart for the day of the hurricane 25th Jan 1990

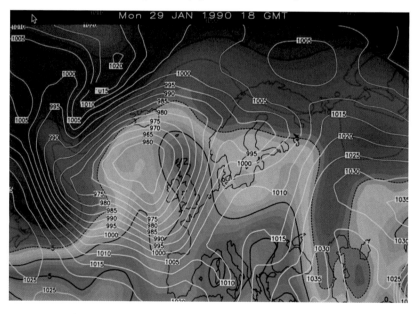

Weather chart for the day of the Flag Theofano sinking 29th Jan 1990.

Courtesy of theweatheroutlook.com (both)

Damaged port lifeboat of Flag Theofano after washing ashore on 30th January

pilot aboard, reported at 0900hrs that they could not find the vessel in the anchorage.

Ironically, we had been called out on the Bembridge lifeboat to another unrelated incident in the Portsmouth area that previous night at 0100hrs to search for an intoxicated swimmer at Southsea. That incident, however, had occurred some 5 hours after the *Flag Theofano* had, unknown to anyone, already capsized. The lifeboat was recalled to Bembridge after the missing person was found safe and well ashore by his friends and it was not until the next morning when the *Flag Theofano's* lifeboat and two bodies were discovered ashore at Hayling Island and West Wittering that there was any indication of the fate of the missing ship. We on Bembridge lifeboat were again launched, rescue helicopters scrambled, and other Navy vessels also joined the search. An oil slick and debris were soon located near the Dean Tail Buoy, along with large air bubbles bursting on the surface. Using the lifeboat graphic echo sounder, we soon located the wreck on the seabed in the area of the oil slick. The echo sounder confirmed a large wreck below, standing 36ft (11 metres) high in a water depth of 72ft (22 metres).

A ship's mooring rope was also found floating on the surface, amongst the large air bubbles and an extensive oil slick. A Navy diver on the Portland R172 helicopter entered the water and attempted to dive, but aborted his dive after descending around

40 feet, as the underwater visibility was totally nil. The diver did, however, confirm that he thought that the floating mooring rope he descended on was still attached to something on the seabed, so we tied a buoy to it. The Queen's Harbour Master (QHM) was advised and mobilised a diving team from Portsmouth with an estimated time on site of 1330 hrs. The sad realisation then set in that the *Flag Theofano* had suddenly foundered or capsized while entering the Solent, but the reason for her loss was not to be established until much later.

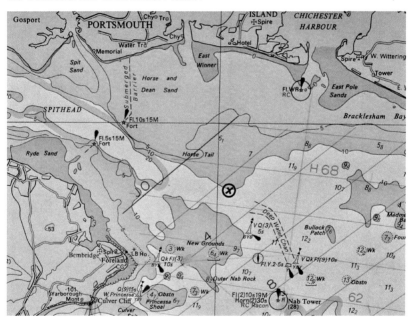

Chart of the area where Flag Theofano sank. Courtesy UKHO

RMAS *Froxfield* left Portsmouth Harbour with a Royal Navy diving team aboard accompanied by the dockyard tug *Rollicker,* which would provide a weather lee for the diving team. Weather on scene was SW force 7 to 8 gusting to 37 knots. The RN diving team reported that it was impossible to dive in the existing conditions and totally nil underwater visibility. They made another attempt the following day with underwater lights and a low-light camera, briefly reaching the seabed, but the Dive Master aborted the dive when the divers said they may as well have their eyes shut in the still totally nil visibility. The RN Dive Master then requested that the helicopter R174 be present overhead for any further diving attempts due to the danger of the task. After several further attempts, a diver secured a line to the wreck on 'something shiny', (which was later proved to be the propellor), as I found that same line wrapped around the propellor when I subsequently dived on the wreck. This line had an underwater sonar reflector arrangement with a buoy on the surface and was attached purely by feel by the RN diver. The part of the sonar line he attached is as illustrated on my diagrams, and was a 5 metre tail line with a thimble eye for attaching to targets located by using sonar reflectors underwater.

Royal Navy Sonar reflector arrangement and surface buoys: Author

The dive master described the diving conditions as 'horrific' and aborted any further attempts. It was decided that as any chance of life on the wreck was now considered impossible, the diving teams were not now prepared to take any more 'calculated risks' with their divers.

A dockyard tug arrived on scene with side-scan sonar equipment borrowed from an RN ship in refit in Portsmouth. An attempt was then made to carry out side scan sonar runs over the wreck on the following day after the sinking, but conditions were still too bad for any stable sonar results to be achieved. Surface swells of 3 metres caused considerable 'cable-snatch', with resultant electronic noise and poor sonar returns. They did, however, get some limited sonar coverage and imagery of the wreck and the adjacent area, but results were understandably poor due to the severe weather conditions.

THV *Patricia* was also mobilised from Weymouth Bay and was on scene early next morning (31st Jan), reporting at 0950 hrs that she confirmed the previous findings of Bembridge Lifeboat, and also that the Dean Tail Buoy had been 'badly collision damaged'.

TIMELINE OF EVENTS

After passing the Nab Tower at 1923hrs and once through the Nab Channel, the *Flag Theofano* would have altered course to port to around 290 degrees towards the Dean Tail Buoy. She was sighted 'making heavy weather' by another ship *Cape Rion,* outward bound north of the Nab Tower. *Flag Theofano* would by then have made her way through the Nab Channel and would be beam on to the heavy southerly/ southwesterly swell and heading towards Spithead and the Solent, intending to anchor in St Helens Roads, as instructed by the Southampton VTS Port Authority.

The light on the Dean Tail Buoy had been damaged in the previous hurricane force winds and it is assumed that the *Flag Theofano* did not see the unlit buoy on radar in the darkness and severe weather conditions. There was also a report that the radar reflector had been blown off the buoy, but this was not definitely confirmed. The Trinity House vessel *Patricia* had been called in after the sinking and, according to the HM Coastguard Incident Action Report, reported that the buoy was 'badly collision damaged'. This was also reported in newspaper accounts, but was later 'quelled' by QHM after they had replaced the buoy, saying that the light had been out of action since the previous Friday, but the buoy was 'not damaged'. This somewhat contradicted the previous reports from THV *Patricia,* HM Coastguard, and local news reports. Unfortunately, I did not get the opportunity to dive on the buoy and chain before it was replaced when the weather conditions allowed. It could well have provided additional clues, but it has to be considered that the weather was far too severe for the unlit buoy to be safely repaired or replaced before the *Flag Theofano* incident occurred. Realistically, in a hypothetical situation of the buoy light failing even an hour before the arrival of the ship, the end result would unfortunately have been the same. I dived on the buoy, chain and sinker shortly after QHM had replaced it and confirmed that all the equipment had been completely renewed.

Later evidence suggests that the crew of *Flag Theofano* probably realised too late that the Dean Tail buoy was very close on their port side and they had tried to turn away to starboard to avoid it. On diving the wreck shortly afterwards, I reported that the rudder on the wreck was turned partially to starboard, when the ship should actually have been starting a turn to port to head west into St Helens Anchorage. This would suggest that the Dean Tail Buoy was by then sighted on the port side of the ship instead of being well clear to starboard. In the process of trying to get clear of the buoy, the ship probably slowed down and brought her engine into neutral to avoid the buoy chain fouling the ship's

Areas of scraping and chipping caused by buoy damaging recent paintwork.

propellor, with the bridge crew possibly out on the port bridge wing trying to see if the buoy was clear of the vessel's stern and propellor. The ship would now have been virtually beam-on to the heavy seas, creating a very dangerous situation with a loss of forward motion and a bulk cement cargo susceptible to shifting with any violent motion. All evidence points to the Dean Tail Buoy and chain getting jammed between the top of the rudder and the hull of the ship, as I found and filmed severe 'metal to metal' fresh rust-free scraping damage on subsequent diving when the underwater visibility had improved.

The five ton seabed sinker and heavy buoy chain of the Dean Tail Buoy would have caused a considerable loading effect, virtually stopping and heeling the ship if she was already out of gear and slowing down when the buoy fouled the rudder. The situation would be worsened if she had still retained some forward motion, which could well have caused the ship to list heavily, causing a rapid cargo shift and instantaneous capsize. This would also explain why there was no time for the crew to save themselves with lifejackets, lifeboats or life rafts.

My side scan sonar results confirm where this happened, as a drag mark can clearly be seen running in a north westerly direction and then curving around to starboard, as per the position of the ship's rudder. The subsequent cargo shift and capsize to starboard was obviously instantaneous, as there was no chance to send a *Mayday*, or any other distress call or signal.

Bulk cement cargo is like a liquid and can easily shift in any extreme rolling motion of the ship. The ensuing capsize was obviously rapid and the majority of the crew below would have had no chance to get on deck before the ship turned over. The bodies found ashore next morning were those of the Captain and Second Mate on bridge watch, and the lack of a *Mayday* call or any distress signals may have been due to them being outside on the port bridge wing trying to see where the buoy was, which was by then probably already scraping down under the port side of the ship with the chain soon to be caught in the rudder. This was concluded on later diving inspections and video filming,

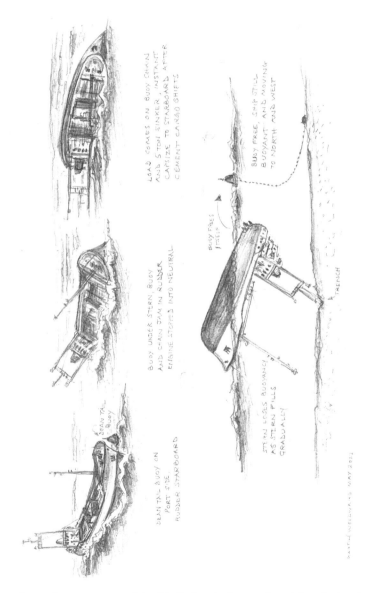

Assumed event sequence of the ship fouling the buoy and capsizing. Author sketch.

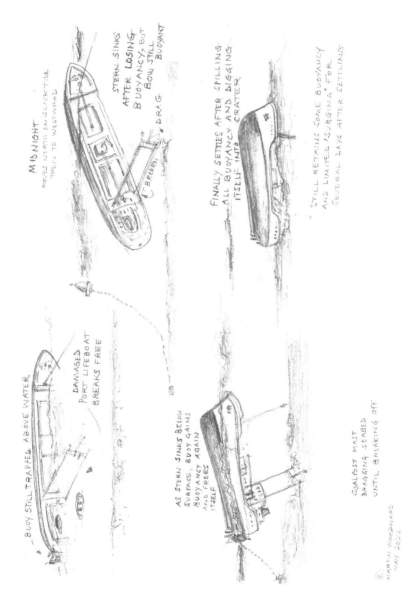

Fig 4. Assumed sequence of Capsize. Author sketch.

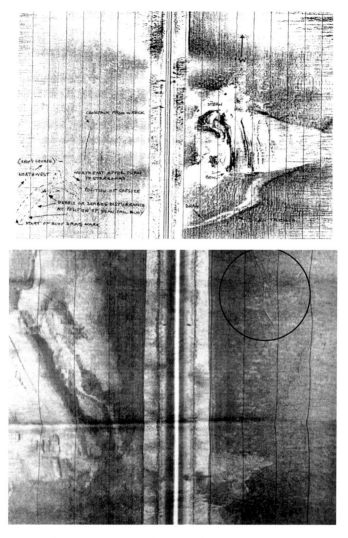

Side-scan sonar images of wreck and adjacent seabed marks.

where clear scraping and damage marks were apparent on what was a recent new paint job on the ship. Most of these damage marks were fresh 'metal to metal' scoring and serious chipping of the paintwork both below and above the water line on the port side, and in particular around the rudder and icebreaking skeg at the stern. These damage marks would also be conducive

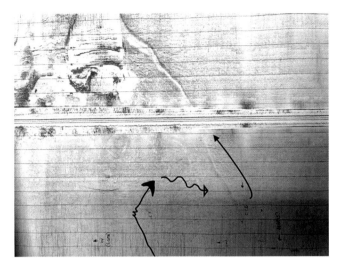

Side-scan sonar images of wreck and adjacent seabed marks.

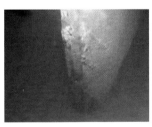

Fresh damage marks on recently painted hull.

with the Dean Tail Buoy causing the horizontal and vertical scrape marks down the port side and stern of the vessel.

The final moments of the *Flag Theofano* were a tragic combination of several factors, which were confirmed by all the evidence gained in later diving and sonar surveys. All indications point to the incident and instant capsize taking place right on the position of the Dean Tail Buoy, with the vessel eventually turning almost upside down and gradually losing any remaining buoyancy over the following hours while dragging along the seabed to where she finally settled. Sonar images confirm the drag track of the vessel on the seabed by the visible trench it caused, and the eventual scour crater it created while

31

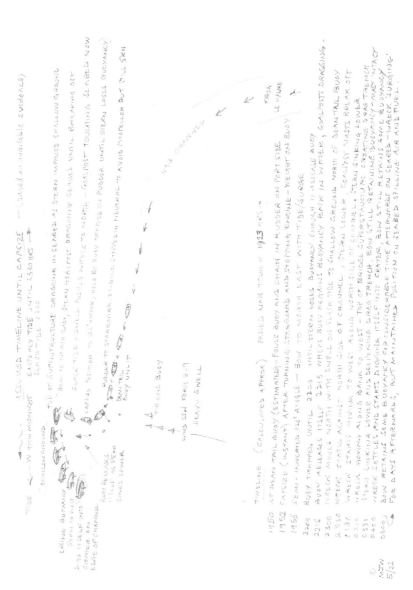

Assumed timeline of events during and after capsize. Author sketch

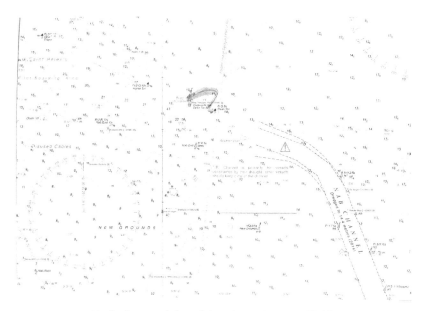

Track of capsized ship while sinking. Courtesy UKHO

finally sliding down the bank and settling into the seabed on the northern edge of the shipping channel.

It was particularly sad that the sinking happened so close to the Bembridge Lifeboat Station, yet there was obviously no time for any distress calls or flares which may have been seen and possibly avoided the tragic loss of all *Flag Theofano's* 19 crew. The irony of the lifeboat being called out to another unrelated incident only hours after the *Flag Theofano* sank was an added tragedy, as if we on the lifeboat crew had been aware of the sinking, we may otherwise have seen something if the timings had coincided.

A 'blame culture' scenario had at first caused debate on who or what was responsible for the sinking, but in reality no specific blame can be attributed to anyone for the tragedy. I will go into the conclusions around that statement at the end of this account.

The wreck of the *Flag Theofano* lies against the northern edge of the main shipping channel into the Solent and Spithead, so it is effectively a navigational hazard to inward and outward shipping for the ports of Portsmouth and Southampton. It therefore now creates a narrower corridor for the bigger ships to negotiate. The Queen's Harbour Master (QHM) wrote to the vessel owners requesting them to remove the wreck as it was a navigational hazard. Tenders were acquired from major salvage companies, but the costs involved were significant and the wreck was later 'abandoned' (a legal term) by the Owners' and insurers due to the financial implications of any salvage operation, which would far exceed the actual value of the ship and her cargo. There was still some responsibility and requirement for the owners to remove the wreck, but the technicalities and logistics of vessel salvage are complex. Much discussion took place between the relevant entities involved, but the difficult decision was then taken by the owners to 'abandon' the wreck. As it was within the legal jurisdiction area of the Queens Harbour Master (QHM) at Portsmouth, it was then left for QHM to attempt the salvage operation to clear the shipping channel. The attempted salvage operation commenced in August 1990, but was abandoned later in the year due to the logistical difficulties involved in removing the already hardened cement cargo, which added a huge amount of weight to the submerged wreck. The allocated budget by HM Treasury to the Navy for the wreck removal was apparently also insufficient to complete the complex salvage operation, hence the *Flag Theofano* still remaining there to this day.

The ship finally settled on the seabed with her bow to the east and stern to the west, orientated approximately 105 degrees/285 degrees. The *Flag Theofano* sadly still remains on the seabed with the bodies of 14 of the Greek, Egyptian and Maldivian crewmen inside.

The bodies of the other five crew and locations where found were as follows;

30th January: Captain (Master) Pittas, Ioannis (Greece: Age 45) West Wittering beach

30th January: Second Officer; Skaltsaris, Hariton (Greece: Age 28) West Wittering beach

14th February: Bosun; Gatanas, Pantelis (Greece: Age 35) Bracklesham Bay beach

16th February: Radio Officer; Frangos, Nikolaos (Greece: Age 37) Selsey, East Beach

19th February: A.B.Seaman; Hussain, Ibrahim (Maldives: Age 19) Bracklesham Bay beach

The locations and timings of the bodies being found are conducive with the Captain (Master) and Second Officer surviving for quite a while after the capsize, as their bodies would not have come ashore so quickly by early next morning at the location they were found if they had drowned immediately after the capsize. It is a strong possibility that as they were both on the bridge when the ship capsized to starboard, they probably clung to the damaged and waterlogged lifeboat that broke away from the port side aft. Their bodies came ashore close together at West Wittering just a short distance east of the upturned lifeboat at East Hayling.

It would seem that when calculating tidal flows and windage factors, along with predicted survival times in January sea temperatures, those two officers most likely succumbed to hypothermia/drowning, sadly perishing when they were nearing East Hayling or West Wittering beach. The inquest stated the cause of death as drowning, which would tie in with the hypothesis above, as they would then be pushed in from not far offshore by the heavy swells in the shallower water. The fairly close proximity of the two bodies at West Wittering to the capsized lifeboat at East Hayling would reinforce this theory, as only Chichester Harbour entrance is between the two positions. The lifeboat was washed ashore upside down and seriously damaged, so it would have been difficult for the Captain and Second Officer to survive for very long in the sea temperatures of that time if they were clinging to the outside of the waterlogged lifeboat.

If they had drowned immediately after the capsize at Dean Tail Buoy, they would (like the other three bodies found much later on) have taken several days to resurface once the decomposition gases in the body eventually provided enough buoyancy to bring them to the surface again, normally several days later in the sea temperatures as they were at that time. Periods of submersion of drowned bodies can obviously vary according to sea temperature winter to summer. By the time the bodies had surfaced and travelled back and forth on the tidal stream, they would have gradually been pushed shorewards by the heavy weather and swells. The timing of when they washed ashore would suggest that the latter three crewmen drowned or succumbed to the cold very quickly, most probably still at the position of the capsize. None of the crew had time to even grab a lifejacket, as none were found on any of the bodies that came ashore. The probable reason that the bodies of the bosun, AB Seaman and Radio Officer did not remain in the capsized ship was most likely because they had just come on watch to prepare to anchor in St Helens Roads. The bosun and AB seaman were possibly already on the foredeck preparing to anchor the ship a short while later, and the Radio Officer (or perhaps one of the bridge crew) had already made a radio call to Southampton VTS a

RN Icosahedron sonar reflector… Photo: Author.

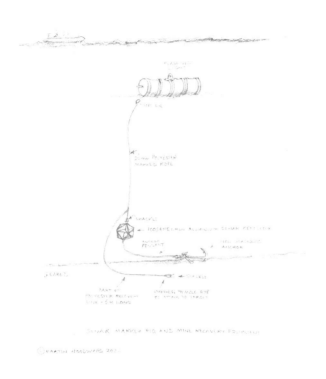

RN Sonar Marker Rig and surface buoy. Author sketch

short time before. The final radio call stated that the ship was passing the Nab Tower at 1923 hrs, and she had also called previously at 1730 hrs, 2 hours before approaching the Nab Tower, giving her ETA at the Nab Tower as 1945hrs.

Subsequent theories and press reports

As with all mysterious disappearances, multiple theories and supposed 'sightings' were soon reported in the media and other sources. When applying even a small amount of logic to these stories, it is simple to eliminate almost all of them immediately. Here are just a few examples, along with logical reasons why they should not even be considered.

A Royal Navy sonar reflector and reel of 20mm diameter rope fouled the propellor, disabling and sinking the ship: Surprisingly, a huge amount of time was spent pursuing this illogical theory put forward by other contractors brought in during the early stages of the diving operation. Based on what they had been told, the Greek Authorities and Vessel Insurers then considered this as a possible contributory factor to the sinking of the ship and subsequently 'abandoned' the wreck for that and other reasons detailed on a previous page. As I was the first diver to actually dive and positively identify the ship as *Flag Theofano,* I was well aware of the rope around the propellor and rudder, as I had seen or felt it when first looking/feeling around the stern gear. I disregarded it as not relevant to the sinking, as I had actually watched the Royal Navy laying those sonar reflectors along with surface buoys *after* the *Flag Theofano* sank. Firstly RMAS *Froxfield* laid a buoy with difficulty, then the minesweeper HMS *Kellington* later guided the RN divers in inflatable Gemini dinghies towards the wreck using those same sonar reflectors suspended on a marked 20mm rope from the Gemini dinghy. The buoys and reflectors fouled the aft end of the ship and a diver attempted to go down, but as mentioned previously, he reported that the underwater visibility was absolutely nil and the sonar reflector and rope were snagged on 'something shiny', which he attempted to tie on to. The diver said it was like having your eyes shut and he could not see anything in the horrific conditions. As diving conditions were so appalling and considered unsafe, the dives were aborted by the RN diving officer. I can well relate to what the diver said, as when I first dived the wreck there was absolutely nil visibility, by far the worst I had ever seen it in decades of diving in this area. Without exaggeration, I had my face mask pressed against the hull with a torch, and could only make out that the hull paint was grey. I actually switched the torch off and spent the rest of that first dive just feeling my way around the capsized wreck, which was still surging and moving at that time with trapped buoyancy. There was obviously still a considerable amount of retained buoyancy in the upturned hull causing the movement. I tapped the hull in several places whilst

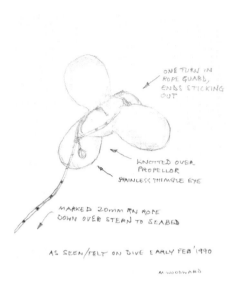

ONE TURN IN
ROPE GUARD,
ENDS STICKING
OUT

KNOTTED OVER
PROPELLOR
STAINLESS THIMBLE EYE

MARKED 20mm RN ROPE
DOWN OVER STERN TO SEABED

AS SEEN/FELT ON DIVE EARLY FEB 1990

M. WOODWARD

Author sketch 1990.

groping around the wreck but, sadly, there was no response.

On subsequent dives I noticed that the rope around the propellor had become more entangled, but there was a simple explanation for that. The 20mm rope was a 'sinking' rope with no buoyancy like a 'floating' rope, therefore every time the tide rose and fell, the rope and buoy would go up and down a few metres and become more entangled around

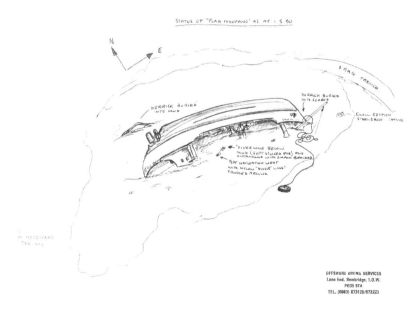

STATUS OF "FLAG THEOFANO" AS AT 1 5 90

N
E

DRAG TRENCH

DERRICK BURIED
INTO MUD

DERRICK BURIED
INTO SEABED

SMALL SECTION
STERN DECK GRATING

"DIVER LINE BELOW
MUD (LOFT STAGES EYE) AND
ENTANGLED WITH SIMON (BRAIDED)
PORT NAVIGATION LIGHT
WITH NYLON "DIVER' LINE'
TANGLED AROUND

M. WOODWARD
FEB 1990

OFFSHORE DIVING SERVICES
Lane End, Bembridge, I.O.W.
PO35 5TA
TEL. (0983) 873125/872223

Author sketch of dive observations after the sinking: Author 1990 the propellor and stern of the ship. This was confirmed by the surface buoys becoming lower and lower in the water until they eventually disappeared completely after the entanglement

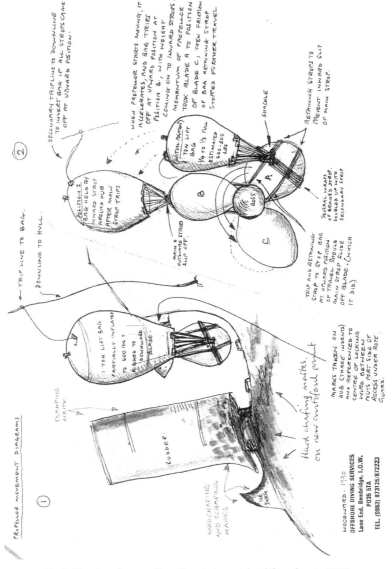

Fig 6. Turning the propellor after rigging with a lifting bag in 1990. Author sketch 1990. (Also repeated on Page 53 as smaller image)

increased on every rise and fall of the tide. Additionally, I later proved that the propellor was in neutral when I rigged a one-ton lifting bag on the downward blade and spun it after inflating the bag with around 600 lbs to 800 lbs of lift. I consulted with several marine engineers over the question of whether the propellor would move if it was still in gear, but the consensus thought not. I also had to research the possible de-clutching aspects, but again, the consensus of engineers were of the opinion that the engine had been stopped and was out of gear. As the ship was 3/4 upside down, surging on the swell and still retaining some buoyancy, the propellor could also have been turning in the tidal stream, which could also explain how the rope wound itself into the shaft more each day.

The configuration and entanglement of the rope changed as time went on, with the sonar reflector (which was previously on the seabed) gradually winding itself further in. The 'thimble eye' tail rope and orientation of the tangle progressively tightened over the stern and down to the seabed. The piece of rope initially looped around the propellor had a spliced eye and thimble … which according the the RN diagram, was the short section for tying or shackling onto a mine or other such sonar target. On my early dives, there was no sign of the sonar reflector anywhere near the propellor, but it gradually wound itself up from the seabed to the propellor over the course of several days. The theory of the rope and sonar reflector causing the ship to sink was totally illogical to say the least, and would be of real concern if the day ever came when a 20mm diameter rope could sink a ship. Having cleared hundreds of ropes from propellors in my diving career, it is always obvious whether the propellor was moving when the entanglement occurred. In this case, the rope was deployed by the RN after the ship had sunk to guide the divers in to the wreck.

***Collision with another ship:** This would have allowed plenty of time for a *Mayday* message, not only from *Flag Theofano* herself, but also from the other ship involved in any supposed collision.

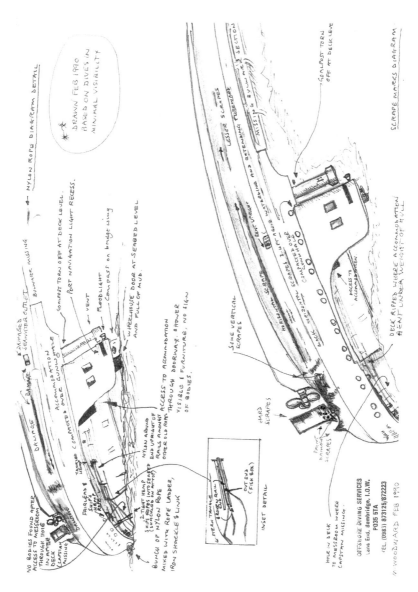

Fig.7 Early dive observations in minimal underwater visibility in February 1990. Author sketch.

*Running aground on Bembridge Ledge and holing the ship:
As this scenario would mean a distance travelled of nearly 4 miles from hitting the ledge to reaching the sinking position, this would allow plenty of time for a *Mayday* distress call and would also have to involve a serious navigational error, which would be highly unlikely. Added to this, the ship was coming from Le Havre, which would require a course of around 337 degrees with a route via the Nab Tower and the Nab shipping channel. This would be some four miles away from Bembridge Ledge.

*Report of 'sighting a ship passing Bembridge Ledge and disappearing shortly afterwards':This report originated from a lady in a house at Forelands, Bembridge who thought she saw a ship close to Bembridge Ledge at around 0100hrs on the 30th January. She stated that the ship passed very close to the ledge and then 'the ship's lights disappeared'. This story is also totally unlikely for the reasons stated in the 'running aground' paragraph above. Additionally, her sighting was some 4 or 5 hours after the *Flag Theofano* had already sunk, and was probably instigated by the coincidental later launching of the Bembridge lifeboat to an unrelated incident at Southsea after midnight. The sound of the lifeboat maroons being fired probably caused the lady to make wrong assumptions about what she thought she had seen.

*Theory that 'a wartime mine could have been dislodged in the extreme weather' (!):

This fanciful and extraordinary theory came from an individual who suggested that a WW2 mine dislodged from the seabed may have blown up the *Flag Theofano* as she came into the anchorage! What makes it more unbelievable was that the statement was made by someone who professed to be a 'Marine Consultant', but he obviously didn't consider that all the ships anchored close by in St. Helens Roads anchorage would have heard and felt the explosion, as would all local residents both sides of the Solent. I live on the seafront at Bembridge overlooking where the *Flag Theofano* capsized, and would certainly have been aware of any such catastrophic explosion, and probably lost a few windows as well!

*Collision with a navigational buoy such as Dean Tail Buoy or New Grounds Buoy:

Even though this was a definite possibility when combined with other factors described later in this account, a collision with a buoy alone is unlikely to cause sudden catastrophic structural damage to a ship. By its very nature, a buoy is circular, and if a ship runs into it, the buoy will almost always roll along the side of the hull. The only real danger from a buoy is getting it fouled around the propellor or rudder and disabling the ship in bad weather. Again, that situation alone with a ship carrying normal cargo would generally give enough time for a *Mayday* distress or *Pan Pan* urgency call to be sent. However, a cumulative sequence of events starting with a collision and entanglement with a buoy, ending with an instantaneous cargo shift capsize is a definite possibility, and one that I will cover in a following paragraph.

The opinion of the majority of people with maritime experience was that the incident had to be catastrophic and instantaneous to prevent the crew from sending a *Mayday* distress call, launching lifeboats or liferafts, or even grabbing lifejackets. The consensus of opinion was that the sinking of *Flag Theofano* was almost certainly caused by shifting of the bulk cement cargo, resulting in an instant capsize within literally seconds. The ship had been loaded in Le Havre a few days previously and been delayed by the storms, so theoretically the cement cargo had plenty of time in the four days delay of sailing to settle, de-aerate and stabilise in the hold before the ship sailed. Due to this delay and time-scale, shifting boards to prevent cargo shift were not considered necessary, and the free surface effect of the cargo was not considered at the time. The ship was also fitted with vibrating pads at the bottom of the holds to speed up de-aeration of the cement. However, when the ship was fully loaded on this final voyage and down to her loadline marks, the cargo holds were apparently only two thirds full, hence there being a large void space above the cargo surface. With no centreline bulkheads or shifting boards fitted, any unpredicted violent ship rolling movements could have caused a rapid shift of the cargo.

As per the MAIB report, despite the cargo effectively trimming itself during the delayed sailing, no further trimming had been carried out, and the loading had been through only one inlet per hold, possibly making the surface profile irregular. In normal circumstances this would not be a problem in reasonable weather conditions, but the weather was still extreme when the ship sailed, with a strong southerly/SSW gale force 9 and heavy seas remaining from the hurricane force winds only four days before. The MAIB report states that bulk cement is known to be a dangerous cargo if there is any space for it to shift in heavy weather, and other ships have been known to have been lost in those very same circumstances. Crossing the English Channel from Le Havre on a course of approximately 337 degrees the seas would have been from virtually astern, but on turning north westward after the Nab Tower, the seas would have been on the beam for a short distance before turning to port after the Dean Tail Buoy to head into the St Helens anchorage.

If the ship had maintained normal forward way on entering the Eastern Solent it should have safely reached the anchorage, but this is where the Dean Tail buoy played a significant part in the sinking. After fouling the buoy down the port side and the chain jamming in the top of the rudder between it and the ice skeg, the ship would have continued to starboard with the stern going to port across the buoy chain. As the tide was flooding to the east at that time, this scenario fits the evidence. My side-scan sonar images confirm this happening right at the Dean Tail Buoy, with the ship now being out of control, trapped by the buoy and continuing to starboard with a beam sea. This, combined with the weight of the buoy, chain and 5 ton sinker would have caused violent motion with an instantaneous shift of the cargo and resultant capsize. That left no time for a *Mayday* distress call, nor getting lifejackets, lifesaving gear, lifeboats or liferafts prepared.

As with other similar capsizes after bulk cement cargo shift, the *Flag Theofano* most probably initially laid over on her starboard side at an angle of between 100 and 120 degrees from vertical, which would still enable the after port lifeboat to break away from its mountings in the heavy seas, before the ship gradually lost further buoyancy at the stern. The retained buoyancy in the ship would explain why it took a few hours to eventually sink some 400 metres west from the capsize position at the Dean Tail Buoy. As previously mentioned, the two bridge crew probably clung on to the damaged and waterlogged port lifeboat as the ship sank, whereas the Bosun and AB seaman on the bow would have been too far away to reach it and were probably washed away from the bow and drowned quickly in the heavy seas. The Radio Officer probably got out from his radio position or the bridge area, but sadly did not make it to the waterlogged lifeboat with the other two bridge crew. He must also have drowned very quickly, as his body was not found until over two weeks later in the same area as the Bosun and AB, whose bodies also came ashore within the same few days in mid-February.

The eventual MAIB and inquest conclusions were that a cargo shift and instant capsize were the prime cause of the tragedy, which was certainly the case. In many incidents though, it is also often an accumulation of events leading up to the end result, and I strongly believe that was the case with this incident.

At this point, I emphasise and reiterate again that my conclusions, assumptions and interpretations of evidence are my own opinions based on all the diving and sidescan sonar investigations I carried out on the wreck after it sank in January 1990. I have a large amount of files on the loss of *Flag Theofano*, and as I live on the seafront at Bembridge overlooking the site to the northeast of my house, I can clearly see the cardinal wreck marker buoys from my windows. As a result of that, I am frequently reminded of the tragedy, and the sad fact that 14 of the crew are still entombed in the wreck. Those 14 crew would have had little or no chance of escape, as the majority of them would most likely have been down below in the accommodation. With the ship capsizing so instantly, their chances of getting out alive were negligible. Mercifully, it was hopefully a quick and painless death for them.

After detailed analysis of all the available information, both at the time of the sinking and many times since, I am confident that the following is what actually happened in the final minutes of the *Flag Theofano.* This is based on solid evidence from my diving surveys, sonar images and other relevant facts.

Relevant points and evidence to consider:

The scraping damage along the port side and around the stern was fresh and back to bare metal, with absolutely no rust formed. The scraping marks above and below the waterline were also conducive with the Dean Tail Buoy and chain impacting along the port side and also scraping vertically up and down at the stern once the ship had the buoy caught between the top of the rudder and the ship's bottom, between the rudder and the ice skeg. One of the vertical struts of the port side sea water outlet was bent and scraped back to bare metal, as were adjacent damage marks along the port side below the water line. Significantly, at one end of the rudder top on the other side of the rudder gland there was a small portion of marine growth/barnacles and old rust where the shipyard workers had not reached when the ship was painted a few months before. The buoy chain had obviously not reached that small area, but the rest of the rudder top was scraped back to clean bare metal.

The paint was also removed back to bare metal on the leading bottom edge of the rudder. As the ship had just been recently painted and anti-fouled, the fresh damage marks were easy to see and identify. Some of the longitudinal marks were typical double chain marks, as would be expected on contact with heavy linked chain. All the impact scraping and marks at the top of the rudder and adjacent ship's bottom are conducive with the buoy being trapped on the port side of the rudder until the ship capsized and it eventually released itself. Bear in mind that when the ship capsized and rolled over to starboard, the bottom of the hull and stern gear would be above water, as would the buoy and chain trapped in the rudder. As the stern settled lower, the buoy would then regain buoyancy and release itself, as the ice skeg and rudder would not then trap the buoy and chain in the same way as when the ship was the normal way up,(see Fig.8). The damage marks all support that theory, as can be seen in the photograph comparing the damaged areas to an undamaged area of the recently painted hull.

If the ship had continued with the kinetic force of a ship of that size under way, the buoy may have been dragged a considerable way, but the actual drag mark (firstly in a north-westerly direction as per the ship's course, then curving to starboard to the northeast after the rudder was turned starboard and engine put in neutral) was only around 45 metres, which would indicate that the buoy chain and 5 ton sinker effectively slowed and heeled the ship if it had still retained reduced forward way through the water. These drag marks are clearly visible on the sonar images, as are the other sonar indications of where and how things happened during the subsequent rapid capsize.

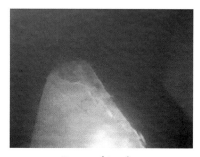

Damaged ice skeg.

Severe scraping damage.

*General condition of hull paint
in undamaged areas.*

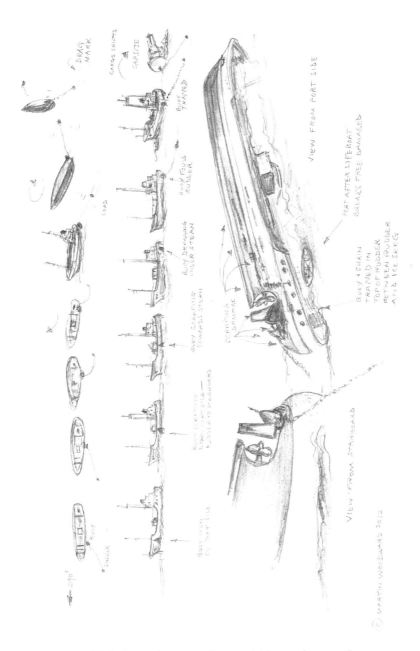

Fig 8. Assumed sequence of events with inverted stern and trapped buoy, viewed from both sides. Author sketch.

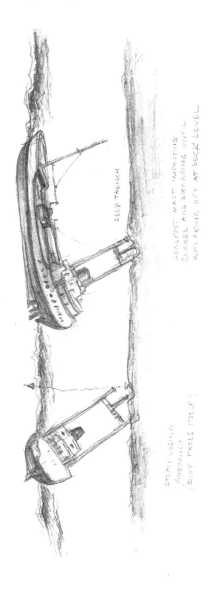

Fig 9. Inverted ship after capsize. Author sketch

CONCLUSIONS

As mentioned previously, there is no intention here to attribute any blame whatsoever, but purely to ensure that what I write is accurate from the relevant aspects of the available evidence. I mentioned all the 'blame culture' issues in previous paragraphs, whereas there is not really any blame attributable to anyone except for a sad twist of fate.

The sinking was an accumulation of unfortunate events that led to the tragic loss of the ship and crew, and I am confident that all the evidence from my involvement in the incident is credible and conclusive. One thing is for sure is that the *Flag Theofano* got caught up in the unlit Dean Tail Buoy, as all the port side damage/scraping to the newly painted hull (below and above the waterline) and around the rudder/skeg and stern area all categorically confirm that. Additionally, I can clearly see the drag marks on my side-scan sonar records where she caught and dragged the Dean Tail buoy while turning to starboard to try to avoid the buoy, and also the fallen debris and associated seabed marks at the position of capsize. All my sonar records confirm exactly where it all happened, and also show the drag trail of the after goalpost masts before they broke off on the shallower ground to the north of the buoy. The deeper superstructure drag mark created after the stern lost further buoyancy and impacted the seabed is also clearly seen on the sonar records. I think the ship would have been initially partially inverted immediately after the capsize, then as the stern lost buoyancy and the tide turned, she gradually moved northward and then westward to her present position around 400 metres away. The bow was obviously the last part to sink after a fair time of spilling buoyancy over a few hours, hence the foremast not breaking off. The wreck was still spilling large air bubbles of buoyancy on the following day, when we and other vessels were there searching for survivors.

As mentioned, the ship was still moving/surging with retained buoyancy when I dived it even days later and the sonar records again clearly show how that retained buoyancy enabled the ship to gradually slip down the bank and dig itself into a large crater, seriously bending and damaging the superstructure. I was at one time a bit concerned about spurious sonar indications created after the event by the actions of QHM's vessels dropping sinkers near the wreck and creating newer seabed marks, but fortunately I later acquired the RN sonar results that were done the following day immediately after the sinking, (before QHM mooring vessels were on site), and the same buoy drag mark is visible on the RN results. These confirm the same drag mark images from the Dean Tail Buoy position as shown on my sonar results. The RN sonar results were understandably poor due to the rough weather, but I could see enough to confirm my own results. I also calculated (by the drag mark directions relative to tidal stream and wave surge) the direction and timings of the ship finally settling on the seabed some hours after the capsize.

I cannot agree on a simple weather knockdown/cargo shift theory, as I was out in the Eastern Solent that night on the Bembridge Lifeboat on an unrelated call-out, and although conditions were very rough, they were not bad enough to capsize a ship of that size if it was still under power and making way through the water. That is where the out-of-gear propellor aspect comes in as yet another relevant piece of evidence that the engine had been stopped into neutral and the rudder turned partially to starboard. As mentioned before, I proved that the propellor was in neutral by turning it with a lifting bag as illustrated in Fig 6. The ship was on a heading of about 290 degrees, shortly about to turn to port to head into St Helens anchorage, and she only had a very short distance to run on that bearing with a beam sea and wind. She would have been on the starboard side of the channel looking out for the unlit Dean Tail Buoy, as presumably the master would have been aware (via a Notice to Mariners) that the buoy had been unlit since four days before. As the ship was on the northern edge of the channel nearer the shallower ground, the swell could have been even worse in that area.

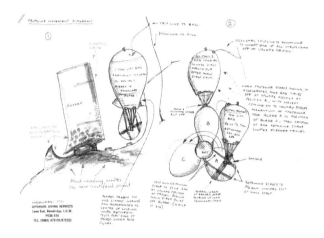

Fig 6. Propeller being turned with lifting bag). Author Sketch.

The only explanation for the ship to be turning to starboard and stopping the engine would be that they saw the buoy coming down the port side and were fearful it may foul the propellor. By turning to starboard when the tide was flowing eastwards, the stern would swing to port and create a slack chain as the ship pushed the buoy into the tide and under the stern. It then got caught between the top of the rudder and hull in the area between the rudder and the ice-breaking skeg, as the fresh paint damage and scraping are clearly visible to confirm that. The ship would then have swung to the northeast (again shown by the buoy drag marks) and been at the mercy of the heavy seas and wind, rolling uncontrollably, or more probably stopped and heeled over by the drag of the buoy and 5 ton sinker, causing the instant capsize.

As also mentioned previously, the sad thing is that the Master and Second Officer almost certainly clung on to the damaged port lifeboat after it broke free, and that explains how they were ashore by early the following morning (30th Jan) when their bodies were found at West Wittering, a short distance east of where the damaged/semi-submerged lifeboat came ashore upside down at East Hayling. They could not have washed ashore there so quickly (and across the tidal stream) unless they were still alive and hanging on to the damaged lifeboat until fairly near to the shore, when they presumably succumbed to hypothermia and drowned shortly before reaching safety. The other three bodies came ashore much later between 14th and 19th February, which would suggest they drowned immediately after the capsize and sank underwater until the normal decomposition gases brought them to the surface much later... as is the usual case. They would then have been subject to tidal and surge conditions and gradually came ashore further to the east. Those three crew were the Radio Officer, Bosun and AB, who would have been on watch and preparing to anchor at St Helens Roads. Sadly, the remainder of the crew were probably trapped down below and had no chance of getting out in time, hence no more bodies of the rest of the 14 crew being found. After the tragedy and on completion of our diving investigations, I made the offer that myself and my diving team could cut an access hole in the hull through to the accommodation to locate and remove the remaining bodies, but sadly my offer was not taken up at the time. Consequently, those 14 crew stayed entombed inside the wreck.

One thing for sure is that the *Flag Theofano* got caught up in the unlit Dean Tail Buoy, as all the port side paint damage/scraping to the newly painted hull (below and above the waterline) and around the rudder/ice-breaking skeg and stern area all categorically confirm that. The fresh 'metal to metal' scraping marks are also evident extending forward to beyond the main engine sea water cooling outlet just below the waterline under the forward end of the superstructure and the bridge wing. These are were all freshly made damage marks at the time of the sinking, as it is easy to differentiate between these and minor older marks and scars that had formed rust beforehand.

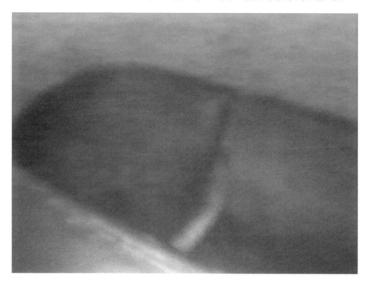

Port side seawater outlet damage.

Another clear indicator is the area of the propellor and stern gland under the rope guard, which was firstly attacked with a hydraulic grinder and then burnt off by the other underwater contractors. This was during their fruitless efforts to attribute and implicate the Royal Navy's sonar buoys and ropes as the reason for the sinking of the *Flag Theofano*. In later removing a section of rope guard with Kerrie Cable (thermic lance) they exposed the underside of the rope guard and shaft area which would have been previously inaccessible to painters during the ship's refit a few months before. As no anti-foul paint had been applied in this section of inaccessible covered area, minor previous marine growth was still present as a thin calcarious covering, which had not been 'shined' by their *accused nylon rope caught in a supposedly turning propelfor'* (according to their incorrect theories). In fact it proved just the opposite, as the only shining was where the bottom rope strands of the nylon sonar rope had 'laid' on the shaft forming a rope pattern, but clearly without the shaft ever turning under power. This is all evident on the underwater video I filmed, as are all the damage marks on the hull and stern area. No growth had formed on the clean propellor or freshly scraped patches of bare metal scraping caused by the buoy since the ship sank.

Clear 'static rope-lay marks' on propeller shaft.

After hearing and reading many different and inaccurate versions of the incident over the last three decades, I decided to write this account to tell the true story of the *Flag Theofano* tragedy based on the evidence detailed herewith. As previously mentioned, I am constantly reminded of the sinking of the ship, as I can clearly see the wreck marker buoys from the windows of my house here on the Isle of Wight. I am therefore also frequently reminded of the 14 unfortunate crew members who still remain entombed in the wreck. As technology has improved dramatically over the last 30 years, I have been back out to the wreck again in my boat to reconfirm a few details and also get some stunning new images with my latest updated down-imaging and side-scan sonar equipment. Whilst there, I also located and accurately pinpointed other pieces of outlying wreckage such as the severed goalpost masts and other items that had fallen off the ship during the capsize. This scatter trail of wreckage and the drag trench again confirm the route of the ship from the point of capsize to the final position of settlement some 400 meters west of Dean Tail Buoy.

As also mentioned earlier, the wreck was 'abandoned' (a legal term in maritime law) by the owners and their insurers in 1990, (see earlier explanations on a previous page), resulting in the Royal Navy/QHM reluctantly taking on the task of attempting salvage or removal. The RMAS salvage vessel *Salmaid* and her diving teams later cut access holes into the cargo hold on the port side of the upturned hull, but the difficulties of the task caused operations to be ceased late in the autumn of 1990. They did their very best in what was a very difficult operation when the cement cargo solidified as it did. The budget for the operation was also apparently insufficient when considering the significant task in hand.

The RN salvage attempts took place from August to October 1990, some months after I had completed all my diving work on the wreck. I did not therefore see or witness any of the results of underwater salvage efforts at that time. Consequently, I can only relate what details were passed on to me. Interestingly, the latest sonar images I achieved in May 2022, (shortly before publication of this book), clearly show the three holes cut into the hull by the salvage divers contracted by the Director of Marine Services (Navy) to the RMAS salvage vessel *Salmaid*. The team apparently included five members of Rosyth Port Diving Group. The first two holes cut were 3ft square and the third was 8ft square, as can be seen in my 2022 sonar images, but it was still not possible to effectively remove any significant quantity of cargo in the difficult circumstances. A specialist barge *Wilcarry 432* was later brought in to carry out borehole drilling of the seabed to ascertain if the area could be dredged and the wreck rolled into a crater. Unfortunately, this idea was also abandoned shortly afterwards due to the logistical difficulties involved.

2022 Sonar imaging showing Flag Theofano upside down on the seabed, with the bridge structure crushed outwards. Photos: Author

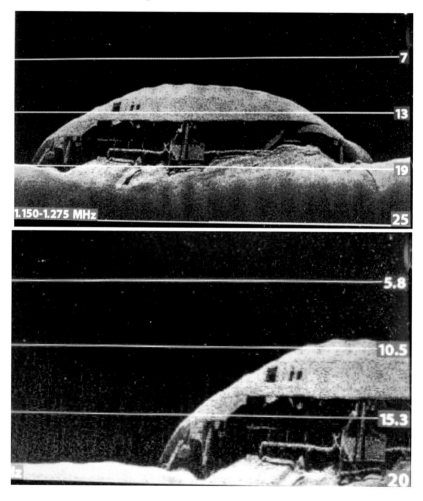

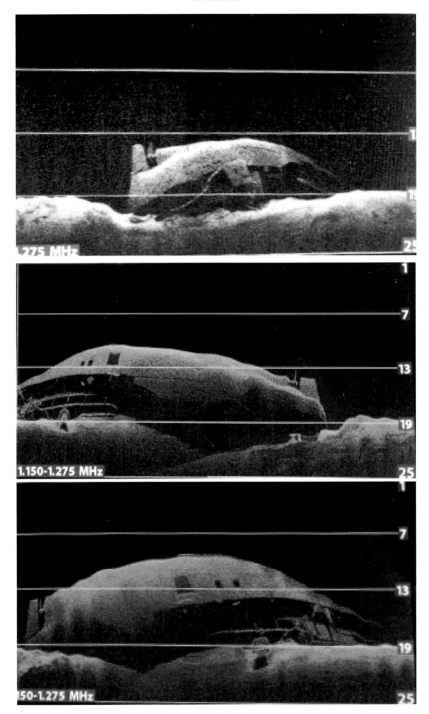

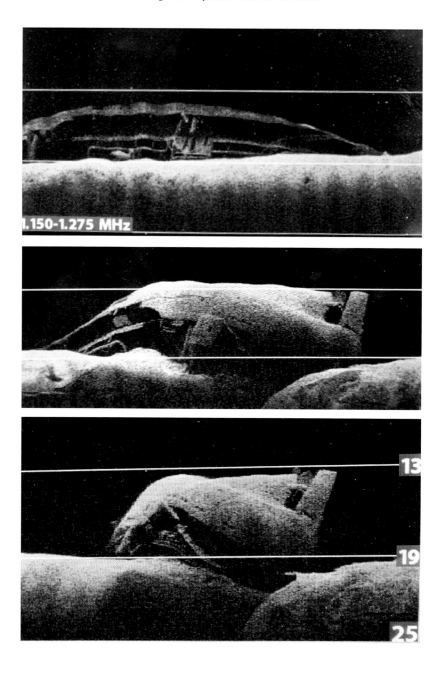

MARINE ACCIDENT INVESTIGATION BRANCH (MAIB) REPORT

(Details courtesy of the MAIB)

Having worked with the MAIB on more than one occasion in the past, I always found them a very capable unit who always viewed all available evidence carefully and objectively. I enjoyed working with them and we had several meetings about the *Flag Theofano* incident. It was certainly not an easy task for them when there was no actual ship to examine, nor any survivors or witnesses.

The MAIB spent several months investigating the circumstances surrounding the loss of the *Flag Theofano,* and examined all available evidence. With so little firm evidence, it was all the more difficult to come to a definitive conclusion without the ship being raised and examined. This was not deemed possible due to the nature of the cargo, the expense of the operation and the logistical difficulties of the task. The MAIB therefore had to consider all the various possibilities to determine the cause of the accident, based purely on available evidence and expert witness testimonies. They carefully scrutinised all details of the 1989 conversion of the ship for specifically carrying bulk cement, which also included fitting angled hopper bottoms to the holds to keep the cargo central and stable. The main holds were also permanently welded and closed off to facilitate installation of bulk cement handling/loading equipment.

The MAIB team visited the cement works in Lafarge Pier, Le Havre to check on the loading records of the *Flag Theofano* prior to her fateful last voyage. The ship had loaded a cargo of 3920 tons of Portland Cement BS12 from a silo at the plant. Both holds were filled at a rate of over 500 tons per hour through single deck inlets, which took approximately 7 hours. Only two inlets had been used and then closed off after loading was completed. The cargo surveyor measured the ship's loadline and draft marks before and after the cement was loaded aboard, and established the total quantity of cargo. After loading, the forward draft was 5.91 metres and the after draft 6.54 metres, which complied with the International Loadline Requirements.

The weather conditions at sea at the time of cargo loading were extreme, with hurricane force winds blowing in the English Channel. This delayed the *Flag Theofano's* sailing for 4 days, as the storm continued and the ship awaited better weather. The Captain decided on the 29th January to set sail for Southampton, and she sailed at 1128 hrs. The French pilot left the ship at 1145 hrs outside Le Havre. The weather forecast broadcast that morning was for a 'southerly gale Force 8 increasing severe gale 9', which was updated at 1305 hrs to 'severe gale Force 9 perhaps storm Force 10 later'. After the pilot had left, there were no further transmissions from the ship until 1730 hrs, when she called Southampton VTS with an ETA for the Nab Tower, which she later passed at 1923 hrs. There were several other transmissions with the Southampton and Portsmouth Port Controls, as the Pilot considered the weather was too severe to safely berth the ship at Southampton, hence requesting at 1840 hrs that *Flag Theofano* go to anchor in St. Helens Roads.

Just before midnight the wind decreased temporarily, and Southampton VTS attempted to call the ship to say that the duty Pilot thought there may be an opportunity to berth the ship, but there was no reply from the *Flag Theofano.* Two more calls were made just after midnight, but again there was no response from the ship.

The next morning, a *Flag Theofano* ship's lifeboat was washed ashore at East Hayling, and two bodies were found at West

Wittering. The duty Pilot reported he could not find the ship in the St Helens Roads anchorage, despite searching and also calling on the VHF radio. Enquiries were then made to the Port Agent to ask if the ship had been unhappy with weather conditions at the anchorage and had remained outside 'slow steaming ('dodging') into the sea until the weather improved. This was considered unlikely given the prevailing storm force conditions, and the realisation quickly set in that something serious had happened to the ship. The rescue services then swung into action, as detailed in previous pages. Weather conditions were at that time SSW Force 8 to 9, increasing to Storm Force 10. A wreck was confirmed after echo-sounding by the Bembridge Lifeboat in the area of Dean Tail Buoy, and an oil slick, ship's rope and other debris sighted. A Portland helicopter diver attempted to reach the wreck via a floating ship's rope attached to the seabed, but had to abort his dive due to the horrendous conditions.

The MAIB followed several lines of enquiry including the following;

Collision with another vessel:

In the absence of any reports of a collision and the lack of any distress calls, this possibility was considered extremely unlikely. Our later diving reports to the MAIB stated that we had not found or felt any visible structural damage to the ship.

Collision with Navigational Buoys:

The MAIB rightfully concluded that an actual collision with a buoy would in itself be extremely unlikely to cause major structural damage to a ship, or cause an immediate sinking preventing any distress calls. Buoys tend to roll alongside a ship and it would be difficult to hole a vessel by direct impact. Although it was stated that the vessel sank at Dean Tail Buoy, and that the New Grounds Buoy had been reported out of position by approximately 350 metres and damaged, the MAIB could, in fairness, only go by the reports they later received from the relevant Buoy Authorities stating that both buoys had been thoroughly inspected with '**no sign of damage or evidence that the vessel collided with either of them'**. This is where the various reports tend to contradict each other, in particular the report from THV *Patricia* after she arrived on scene, which was also quoted word for word in the Coastguard Incident Report. Perhaps it comes down to individual interpretation as to how comments such as *'badly collision damaged'* can later become *'no damage'*. Buoys do often come into contact with ships and also get moved by storms, so there is inevitably superficial damage to them at times, but the conflicting reports after the *Flag Theofano* sinking did tend to 'muddy the waters' more than a little. Perhaps the emphasis was more on reporting serious 'impact denting' rather than possible 'entanglement damage', which would have appeared less serious.

As mentioned previously, Dean Tail Buoy was removed and replaced as soon as the weather allowed, and I did not get the opportunity to dive and examine it and the chain until after it was all renewed. It would appear that the MAIB possibly did not get the opportunity to inspect it either, but they had a lot of other investigative tasks on at the time and understandably had to rely on the reports they received from the relevant authorities.

Unlit buoy 'may have holed ship'

SPECULATION was growing today that an unlit navigational marker buoy may have holed the Greek freighter which sank off Portsmouth with the loss 19 lives.

The five-ton Dean Tail Buoy was found badly damaged after the tragedy which claimed the Flag Theofano.

The Queens Harbourmaster for Portsmouth, Capt. James Chestnutt, said the buoy had been unlit since Friday, but stressed that it would have showed up on radar.

The Flag Theofano had been en route from Le Havre to Southampton, carrying a cargo of 4,000 tons of cement, and had been due to arrive at 7.45 p.m. on Monday.

But about 5.30 p.m., the last radio contact, her captain was advised against entering Southampton and to seek shelter from the storms off the Isle of Wight.

Coastguards are baffled about how the 300ft. vessel sank so quickly that there was not time to make a Mayday distress call.

Theodore Vanianis, Managing Director of Golden Union, the ship owners, has called for an investigation into why the vessel was told to ride out in the Solent instead of getting a pilot to guide it into port.

A post mortem examination

was being held today at St Richard's Hospital, Chichester, on the ship's master and second mate, whose bodies were washed ashore at West Wittering.

Capt. Chestnutt said the wreck, which lies in busy shipping waters between the Isle of Wight and Portsmouth, is impeding shipping.

"It is the fact that it restricts the width of the channel, and therefore the freedom of movement in this port, that makes me want it gone," he said.

A Royal Naval spokesman said the ship's owners would be required to move the wreck at their cost.

News coverage after the sinking

Overcome by weather:

The *Flag Theofano* was a well-built ship constructed for voyages in ice conditions. As stated previously, she had undergone a complete conversion only a few months before her loss, and the main hatches had been welded to form watertight holds for carrying bulk cement cargo. The MAIB correctly reported our findings underwater that there was *'no weather induced structural damage that could have caused the sinking'* … but that the possibility could not be entirely eliminated. As the starboard side of the ship was partially buried, we could not access some of that part of the hull. Although there was indeed no significant structural damage visible that would have caused the sinking, there was considerable fresh paint damage and scraping to bare metal down the port side and around the stern area and rudder of the ship. This was entirely conducive with the *Flag Theofano* getting caught up in the Dean Tail Buoy, as described in earlier paragraphs of this book. I filmed all the damage once the underwater visibility had improved, and as the ship had only been freshly repainted a few months before, it was easy to determine that the damage marks had only just occurred. No rust had formed, and the 'metal to metal' scraping was back to bare metal, mainly below the waterline and stern gear where normal 'docking scars' could not reach.

As I was reporting to both the MAIB and also the vessel owners/ insurer's representative at the time, I submitted my diving reports and drawings to both parties. It has to be remembered that there was some speculation at the time of who, or what, (if at all) could be blamed for the loss of the ship, with illogical accusations that a '20mm nylon rope and sonar reflector' (laid by the RN *after* the wreck had sunk) may have caused the tragedy. Inevitably, it was later proved by myself and other inquest witnesses that the rope and sonar reflector were put there after the ship had sunk, and therefore had no bearing on the sinking.

Grounding:

Again, the MAIB report correctly states that the diving inspections we carried out did not find any indication of the ship running ashore on Bembridge Ledge or in the New Grounds area. They gave other reasons for grounding being an unlikely scenario, such as lack of distress calls and the distance travelled to the sinking position. A larger ship with a deeper draft had also passed through the area west of the Nab Channel shortly beforehand without any problem. The MAIB also reported on the seabed drag marks we had found that were caused by the after goalpost masts of the inverted ship before it finally came to rest. These are clearly shown on my side-scan sonar records shown in the illustrations .

Loss of Propulsion:

The MAIB correctly state in their report that the rope and sonar reflector wrapped around the ship's propellor could only have got there after the ship sank. Evidence showed that the RN divers had deployed this equipment to assist in homing in on the wreck to carry out their intended dives. The rope was subsequently looped around the propellor in minimal underwater visibility and became more entangled over the following days (see previous paragraph earlier). The MAIB then go on to say that loss of propulsion power due to other failures could not, however, be ruled out.

Loss of Steering

The MAIB state in the report that loss of steering could have been a cause of the loss of the vessel, as it would then have been at the mercy of the severe weather and sea conditions prevailing at the time. Any severe motion could have caused the cement cargo to shift and result in an immediate capsize.

Cargo Shift:

The MAIB then go into the details of the IMO (International Maritime Organisation) Code of Practice for bulk cargoes such as cement. They quote the criteria on required times for the cargo to settle and de-aerate before the vessel leaves port, also loading/ trimming considerations and other aspects. Due consideration and allowance should also be given to ship stability and possible free surface effect. According to the MAIB report and the ship's stability book of the *Flag Theofano,* no account of the free surface effect of the cargo was considered at the time. As the ship was delayed by 4 days due to severe weather, the requirement for 12 hours cargo settlement was well complied with, and the ship also had vibrating pads at the bottom of the hold to assist with settlement. This meant that the fitting of shifting boards was not deemed necessary at the time.

The MAIB also state the important fact that although the ship was fully loaded down to her loadline marks, the cargo holds were only two thirds full. This would have left a large void space above the surface of the cargo and in any situation of extreme motion of the ship could have caused the cargo to shift. No trimming had taken place and the cargo was loaded through only one inlet per hold. This would create the possibility that the surface profile of the cement could have been irregular. The report suggests that on approaching the Dean Tail Buoy to head into St Helens Roads, the ship would have been beam-on to the heavy seas and violent rolling was a possibility. *Flag Theofano* was also seen by another ship *Cape Rion* making 'heavy weather' near the Nab Tower. As other ships carrying bulk cement had suffered cargo shift and capsize, the MAIB carried out thorough investigations and research into the stability of bulk cement. This research concluded that under heavy weather situations and violent ship motion, it was possible for cement cargos to shift, and the report gives the data relevant to certain criteria. With a trimmed cargo, the approximate angle of failure would be around 25 degrees, whereas with an untrimmed cargo, the angle of failure could be as little as 10 degrees with any violent rolling of the ship.

The conclusions and findings of the MAIB report ruled out any collision with another vessel or navigational buoys, or by grounding. Other causes such as being overcome by weather, loss of propulsion or loss of steering remained open to speculation, but were not in isolation considered to be the likely cause of the sinking.

The final conclusion of the MAIB was that the most likely cause of the *Flag Theofano* sinking was a cargo shift as a result of the extreme weather and heavy seas at the time. This could also have been exacerbated by a possible loss of propulsion or steering.

Cargo shift was the consensus opinion of the majority of experts and is definitely what happened. But, as with all accidents, it is often an accumulation of events leading to the final outcome. As explained in my observations and conclusions earlier in this book, all the evidence from my diving and survey work point to the ship fouling the unlit Dean Tail Buoy in her rudder, which then caused the subsequent rapid capsize.

FLAG THEOFANO
INQUEST JULY 1991:
(Courtesy of the Chichester Coroners Office)

As with any incident or accident involving loss of life, an inquest had to be held after all the necessary investigations had been completed. This inquest took place in July 1991, more than a year after the *Flag Theofano* sank. Those of us involved in the investigation of the sinking all attended as witnesses, as did representatives of the MAIB, HM Coastguard, Port Authorities, QHM, the Port Agent and other relevant parties. I was impressed with the Coroner Mark Calvert-Lee and his staff, as the whole thing was handled both professionally and delicately. The Coroner's subsequent report was extremely well-informed and sensitive to the tragic loss of life within Solent waters. Again, the final conclusions had to be reached on what evidence was available, and with no survivors or witnesses this was a difficult task. If the ship had been recovered, this could have provided many more clues, but despite the lack of significant evidence the Coroner handled the whole thing superbly.

The first part of the inquest involved examining evidence surrounding the finding of the bodies, their subsequent identification and then the post mortem and medical examinations to determine the cause of death. The opinion of the Consultant Pathologist was that all five bodies found died by drowning and all these aspects of the deaths were handled with sensitivity.

This was then followed by evidence from the MAIB, duty watch officer from HM Coastguard, the Captain in charge of the Port of Southampton, and the duty Pilot. After that, it was the turn of the Queen's Harbour Master to give his evidence, then myself to give details of the weather conditions in St Helens Anchorage during our unrelated lifeboat callout on the night of the sinking. I then gave evidence of my diving work, underwater findings, including the damage marks on the hull, and my opinion of the illogical 'rope theory'. Next in line was the RN/QHM officer in charge of Marine Search and vessel designation. He gave details of the vessels involved, the reasons for deployment of the sonar reflector, and other assets assigned to the incident. He was followed by the diving officer from HMS *Kellington*, who also stated that the rope and sonar reflector were deployed by them while attempting to dive on the wreck. The Shipping Agent from Wainwrights was also called to give evidence, as was the Captain of the Trinity House vessel *Patricia,* who was questioned about navigational buoys. He gave details about the New Grounds and other buoys, stating that some 20 of their navigational buoys had been moved out of position by the extreme weather at the time the *Flag Theofano* sank.

The Coroner then explained the various options of verdict based on the available evidence, which could realistically only come under the categories of 'Accident', 'Misadventure' or the lesser possibility of an 'Open Verdict'. He carefully explained to the jury the available options and the difference between 'Accident' and 'Misadventure' verdicts. The way he handled the whole inquest proceedings was very professional.

The jury then retired and returned later with a unanimous verdict of 'Misadventure'. The Coroner then thanked the jury and all the witnesses for their contribution to the Inquest.

Interestingly, the Queen's Harbourmaster came up to me at the end of the inquest and thanked me for dismissing the illogical 'rope theory' about the Royal Navy sonar deflectors and ropes having played any part in the loss of the ship.

Diver sinks rope theory

PROFESSIONAL diver Martin Woodward put an end to speculation that a naval rope had played a part in the sinking of the Greek freighter Flag Theofano.

A pilot at the Chichester inquest into the loss of her 19-man crew, told how he had been ready and waiting to bring the ill-fated vessel into dock.

And the Queen's Harbourmaster at Portsmouth revealed that tapes which could have held information on the tragedy had failed to record its communication channels.

For months after the Theofano slipped into the depths of the Solent on a January night last year, many clung to the theory that a discarded rope had fouled the ship's propeller.

But Martin Woodward, diver and second coxwain on the Bembridge lifeboat, told an inquest jury yesterday the rope had been left after the vessel had sunk.

"To me there was no way this rope had got entangled around the propeller while it was still going," he said.

"If the propeller had been going round it would have damaged the rope."

Freighter theory settled

Professional diver Martin Woodward put an end to speculation that a naval rope had played some part in the sinking of the Greek freighter Flag Theofano.

And more than 20 witnesses have told a Chichester inquest this week their recollections of what happened when the ship's 19 man crew lost their lives on a stormy night in January, last year.

Five seaman, including the ship's captain Ioannis Pittas, were washed up on West Sussex beaches.

West Wittering dog walkers Desmond Moore, of Eton Drive, and Kathleen Bartram, of Spur Point, discovered bodies the day after the ship disappeared into the Solent off the Isle of Wight.

Divers hold clue to mystery of freighter sinking

ONLY divers can solve the mystery of why the Flag Theofano sank to the bottom like a stone – without even a Mayday signal.

That is the opinion of the salvage expert who serves aboard Bembridge Lifeboat, which was first to pinpoint the position where the Greek-registered freighter went down.

Second coxwain of the Bembridge Lifeboat, Martin Woodward, said: "It is a real mystery. You would normally expect some signal, but nothing was heard, nothing at all.

"The only clues to the ship ever having been there that we found were a rope and a slick of diesel fuel. We were able to tie a marker buoy to mark the spot for divers later on.

"I am not prepared to speculate what could have gone wrong, but a ship of her size

should have been easily able to cope with the conditions in The Solent that night.

"When we were called there was a 10ft, swell and we were just about to set off on an exercise so we were at the scene very quickly.

"The position we found her in is about a quarter mile west of the Dean Tail Buoy which is about three miles out of Bembridge and four from Hayling Island.

"We spent about five hours looking for survivors but found nothing."

Mr. Woodward, a former North Sea saturation diver, who is one of the foremost wreck diving and salvage specialists, said: "If I was asked I would welcome the opportunity of diving on the Flag Theofano, in order to help solve the mystery of why she went down in this strange way."

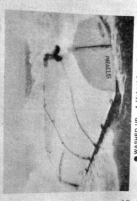

● WASHED UP – A lifeboat from the ship.

News coverage during and after the Flag Theofano sinking and subsequent inquest

Diver has solved sinking mystery

BEMBRIDGE diver Martin Woodward believes he has discovered what caused the sudden sinking of the Greek cargo ship Flag Theofano with the loss of all 19 crewmen.

He told the County Press, "I have inspected the wreck and feel pretty sure I know what caused this tragedy, but the insurers have asked me to keep this confidential for the time being."

Mr Woodward's discovery could provide the vital clue in a Department of Transport investigation which has been under way since the 1,185-tonne vessel vanished in the Solent on the night of January 29 without sending out a Mayday distress call.

The ship was thought to have last been seen close to Bem-bridge Ledge at 1 am, and later was located sunk in the Dean Tail Buoy area near St Helens Roads.

Courtesy of Isle of Wight County Press.

The wreck of the Flag Theofano sleeps on undisturbed, apart from the constant shipping traffic that passes very close to the wreck every day. Hopefully, this small book will contribute to keeping the story alive and commemorate the 19 crew lost in the Solent's worst modern-day shipping tragedy.

ACKNOWLEDGMENTS

I would like to thank the following people for their help in various ways towards this publication and also organisation of the commemoration events, seafront and other memorials, and the headstone for the previously unmarked grave of Ibrahim Hussain in Portsmouth.

Roger Thornton FICS: Wainwrights Shipping Agents, Southampton, who played a major role as Port Agent after the tragedy. Many thanks for all his kind help and advice. Also to his colleagues at the Southampton Shipowners Association who, along with Roger, also kindly contributed to the Ibrahim Hussain headstone .

Steve Hunt, Southsea, for his recent dedicated research and interest in the *Flag Theofano*, also for considerable input on the commemoration events for the crew.

Cllrs Gerald Vernon Jackson, Stephen Baily and David Evans, of Portsmouth City Council for all their help, and also those in PCC that waived charges and gifted the grave site of Ibrahim Hussain to enable a headstone to be legally installed.

The *Chichester Coroner*, for agreeing to share the inquest summary

Louise Cane, Coroners Office, Chichester for all her kind help with the inquest details

Monumental Stonemasons: Alver-Stones of Portsmouth for their kindness and help

The **Rt. Hon Penny Mordaunt MP and Daniel Wemyss**

Simone Dickens: Coco Design, IOW, who always comes up with great advice and assistance when I need it!

Back Cover:

Main Photo: *Flag Theofano* pictured with a piece of the recovered concrete cargo. Photo: Roger Thornton FICS

Bottom right photo of author: Julian Winslow

Other books by this author;

'Bembridge Lifeboat Station...A Village Commitment' 2016

'Bembridge in Old Picture Postcards' 1991